THE SHROPSHIRE
COLOURING BOOK

First published 2016

Reprinted 2019

The History Press
The Mill, Brimscombe Port
Stroud, Gloucestershire, GL5 2QG
www.thehistorypress.co.uk

British Library Cataloguing in Publication Data.
A catalogue record for this book is available from the British Library.

ISBN 978 0 7509 6808 9

Cover colouring by Lucy Hester.
Typesetting and origination by The History Press
Printed and bound by Imak, Turkey

THE SHROPSHIRE
COLOURING BOOK

PAST AND PRESENT

Take some time out of your busy life to relax and unwind with this
feel-good colouring book designed for everyone who loves Shropshire.

Absorb yourself in the simple action of colouring in the scenes and settings
from around the county of Shropshire, past and present. From iconic
architecture to picturesque rolling hills, you are sure to find some of your
favourite locations waiting to be transformed with a splash of colour.

There are no rules – choose any page and any choice of colouring pens or pencils
you like to create your own unique, colourful and creative illustrations.

Weston Park, Shifnal ▸

Castle Gates House, Shrewsbury ▸

Much Wenlock Priory ▸

Dudmaston Estate, Bridgnorth ▸

Church Street, Shifnal ▸

T.V.
Opticians
RESTAURANT
DELI

The Dingle, Quarry Park, Shrewsbury ▸

Severn Valley Railway ▸

7802

Hodnet Hall Gardens, Market Drayton ▸

Ludlow ▸

Buttercross
Market
St Laurence's Church
County Court Library
Broad Gate
Ludford Bridge
SALE
FINAL REDUCTIONS

Oswestry, 1960s ▸

AGRICULTURAL ENGIN

The Shropshire Bedlams ▸

Bridgnorth ▸

Tiles at Jackfield Tile Museum ▸

Wollerton Old Hall Garden ▸

Dorothy Clive Garden, Market Drayton ▸

Greenhouse at Sunnycroft, Wellington ▸

Tyrley Top Lock, Shropshire Union Canal ▸

ARKHOLME

Bridgnorth Castle Hill Railway, Bridgnorth ▸

Shrewsbury Museum & Art Gallery ▸

Shrewsbury School and Boathouse ▸

The tree house at Pitchford Place ▸

Castle Street, Shrewsbury, 1962 ▸

OLIVERS
MARKS & SPENCER

Paragliding at The Long Mynd ▸

Fron Wood ▸

RAF Museum, Cosford ▸

GAR
1
HANGAR
1
TX 214
AIR FORCE

Stokesay Castle, Ludlow ▸

The Wrekin, Telford ▸

Horses at Acton Scott Historic Working Farm, Ludlow ▸

Buildwas Abbey ▸

Iron Bridge, Ironbridge ▸

Attingham Hall, Shrewsbury ▸

‘Awful Precipe’, Hawkstone Park ▸

Shrewsbury Castle and Shropshire
Regimental Museum, Shrewsbury ▸

Worfield, 1905 ▸

Willstone Hill, near Church Stretton ▸

Ellesmere ▸

LEO

Ludlow Castle ▸

Coalbrookdale ▸

Telford sign ▸

The dovecot at Benthall Hall ▸

Wroxeter Roman City ▶

Blists Hill Victorian Town, Ironbridge ▸

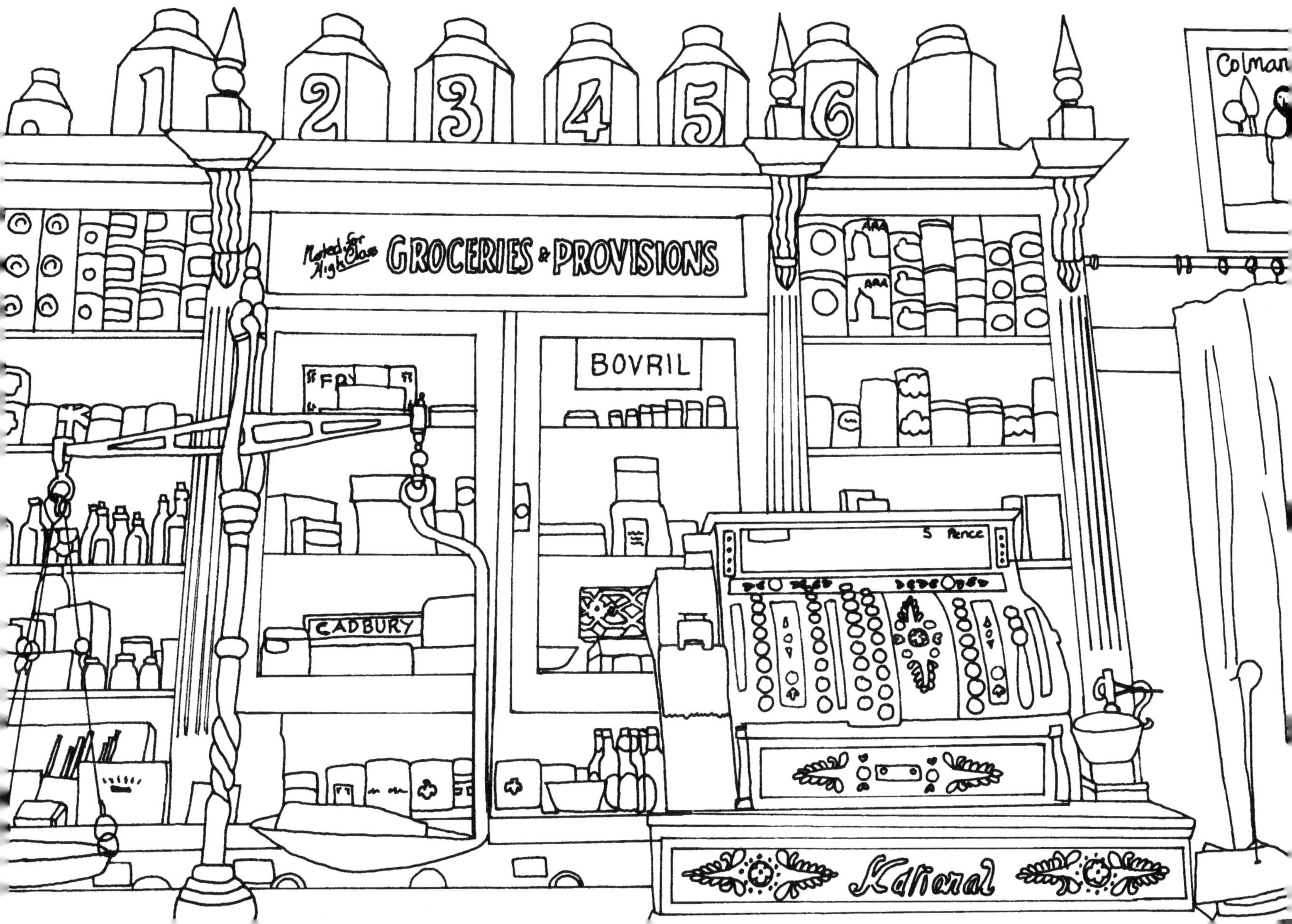
1
2
3
4
5
6
Colman
Noted for High Class
GROCERIES & PROVISIONS
BOVRIL
FRY
CADBURY
5 Pence

Butterfly, The Long Mynd ▸

The Porch House, Bishop's Castle ▸

St Alkmund's Church, Whitchurch ▸